AQUEDUCT OF SEGOVIA

BY BRIENNA ROSSITER

Apex is distributed by North Star Editions:
sales@northstareditions.com | 888-417-0195

Produced for Apex by Red Line Editorial.

Photographs ©: Shutterstock Images, cover, 1, 4–5, 6–7, 8, 9, 10–11, 12, 14–15, 16–17, 18–19, 20–21, 22–23, 24, 25, 27, 29

Library of Congress Control Number: 2023910808

ISBN
978-1-63738-745-0 (hardcover)
978-1-63738-788-7 (paperback)
978-1-63738-872-3 (ebook pdf)
978-1-63738-831-0 (hosted ebook)

Printed in the United States of America
Mankato, MN
012024

NOTE TO PARENTS AND EDUCATORS

Apex books are designed to build literacy skills in striving readers. Exciting, high-interest content attracts and holds readers' attention. The text is carefully leveled to allow students to achieve success quickly. Additional features, such as bolded glossary words for difficult terms, help build comprehension.

TABLE OF CONTENTS

CHAPTER 1

WATERWAY

A stone structure runs through the city of Segovia, Spain. It looks like a huge bridge. But it is part of an **aqueduct**. A **channel** along the top carries water.

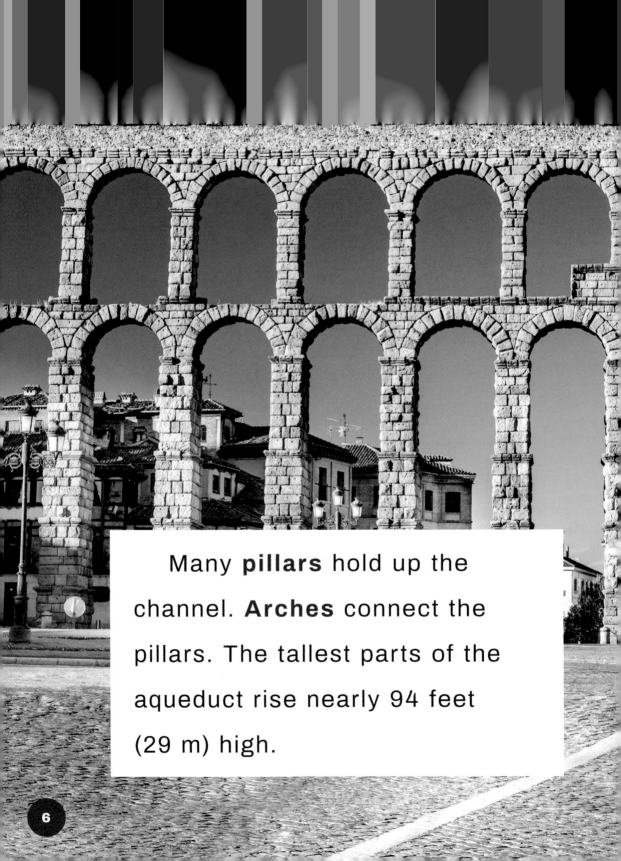

Many **pillars** hold up the channel. **Arches** connect the pillars. The tallest parts of the aqueduct rise nearly 94 feet (29 m) high.

FAST FACT

Only part of the aqueduct is visible. The rest is underground.

The aqueduct has more than 160 arches.

Historians think the aqueduct was built nearly 2,000 years ago.

The aqueduct is an impressive example of **engineering**. It's also very old. Many people come to see it each year.

HISTORIC CITY

Segovia is home to many famous buildings. One is a castle called the Alcázar. Another is a church from the 1500s. The aqueduct is even older.

Secret passages connect the Alcázar to other parts of Segovia.

CHAPTER 2

HOW IT WORKS

Aqueducts carry water. They can use bridges or channels. The aqueduct in Segovia was built to move water from the Frío River to the city.

Aqueducts carry water long distances so that people

First, water flows through a channel in the ground. It travels more than 10 miles (16 km). An intake point connects this channel to the aqueduct's bridge section.

KEEPING CLEAN

Near the intake point, the water flows through a tank. The tank is inside a small building. It helps filter out leaves and debris. That way, the city gets clean water.

The aqueduct's bridge is more than 2,300 feet (700 m) long.

From there, water flows through a channel on top of the bridge. The channel has a slight slope. That keeps the water moving.

The city of Rome also had aqueducts. They supplied water for fountains, baths, and toilets.

FAST FACT

The aqueduct brought water to Segovia for more than a thousand years.

CHAPTER 3

HOW IT WAS MADE

The Roman Empire formed more than 2,000 years ago. It took over much of Europe. Romans were skilled builders. They built the Aqueduct of Segovia around 100 CE.

Workers cut and stacked granite stones to make the aqueduct.

The aqueduct is built from large stones. No **mortar** holds them together. Instead, builders stacked the stones very carefully.

FAST FACT

The aqueduct is made of about 24,000 large stones.

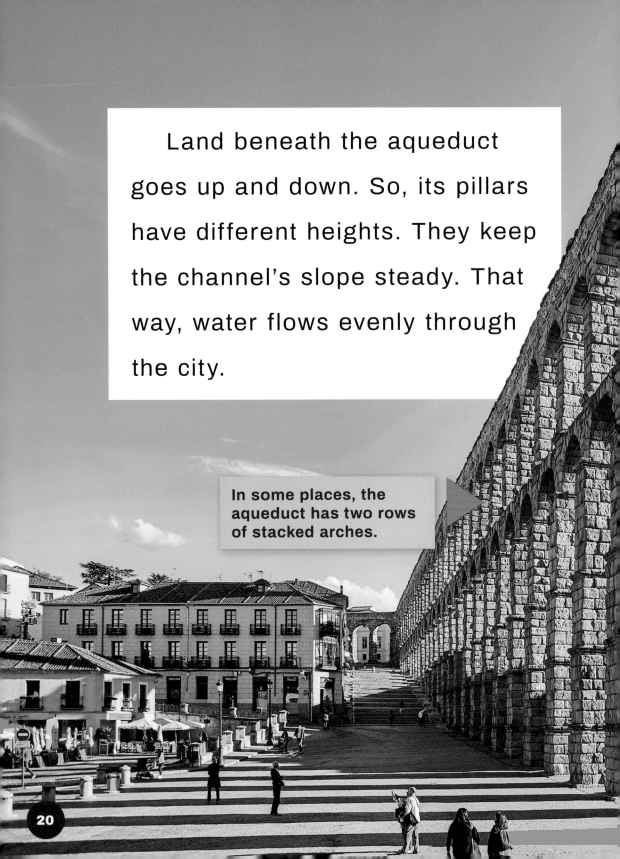

Land beneath the aqueduct goes up and down. So, its pillars have different heights. They keep the channel's slope steady. That way, water flows evenly through the city.

In some places, the aqueduct has two rows of stacked arches.

MAKING CURVES

Builders used wood frames to make the arches. Each frame was a half circle. Builders placed stones along the top. Then, they removed the frame. The stones pressed together to keep the curved shape.

CHAPTER 4

STILL STANDING

The aqueduct supplied water to Segovia into the 1900s. By then, it had some leaks. Parts were also wearing away. So, the city got a new water system.

In the early 2020s, more than 50,000 people lived

Although the aqueduct still stands, people in Segovia no longer use it for water.

Today, the aqueduct is a historic site. It is the largest Roman aqueduct still standing. Most of the original bridge remains.

OTHER AQUEDUCTS

The Romans built many aqueducts. The biggest one was in Carthage. It used to carry water for 80 miles (129 km). But parts of it fell down.

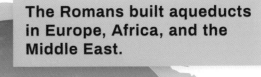

The Romans built aqueducts in Europe, Africa, and the Middle East.

Because they are stacked without mortar, the stones can shift. That helps the bridge survive wind and earthquakes. People also work to **preserve** it.

FAST FACT

Cars once drove under the arches. The **vibrations** caused damage. So, people moved the road.

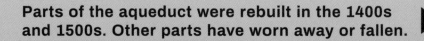

Parts of the aqueduct were rebuilt in the 1400s and 1500s. Other parts have worn away or fallen. ▶

COMPREHENSION QUESTIONS

Write your answers on a separate piece of paper.

1. Write a few sentences describing how the Romans built the aqueduct in Segovia, Spain.

2. If you went to Segovia, which structure would you most like to see? Why?

3. When was the aqueduct built?

    A. around 100 CE

    B. the 1500s

    C. the 1900s

4. How would vibrations from cars damage the aqueduct's arches?

    A. Vibrations would make the arches less stable.

    B. Vibrations would make the arches look bad.

    C. Vibrations would hold up the arches.

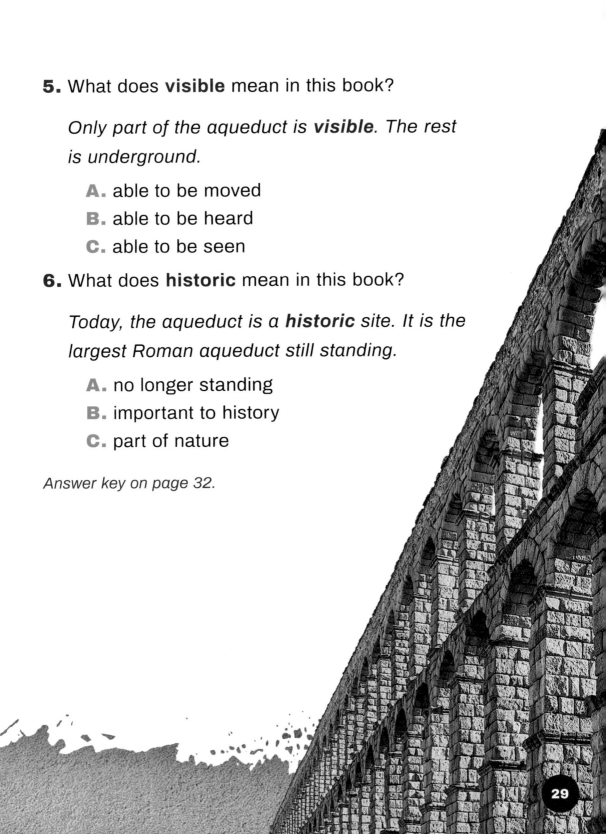

5. What does **visible** mean in this book?

*Only part of the aqueduct is **visible**. The rest is underground.*

    A. able to be moved
    B. able to be heard
    C. able to be seen

6. What does **historic** mean in this book?

*Today, the aqueduct is a **historic** site. It is the largest Roman aqueduct still standing.*

    A. no longer standing
    B. important to history
    C. part of nature

Answer key on page 32.

GLOSSARY

aqueduct
A system that carries water.

arches
Curved parts of structures that go above openings and can help provide support.

channel
A long, narrow dip or cut, often one water flows through.

debris
Pieces of something that broke or fell apart.

engineering
Using math and science to build things and solve problems.

mortar
A material that holds bricks or stones together.

pillars
Tall poles used to support a structure.

preserve
To stop harmful changes from happening to something.

vibrations
Tiny back-and-forth movements.

TO LEARN MORE

BOOKS

Andrews, Elizabeth. *The Ancient Romans*. Minneapolis: Abdo
  Publishing, 2023.

Bowman, Chris. *Bridges*. Minneapolis: Bellwether Media,
  2019.

Gaertner, Meg. *Stonehenge*. Mendota Heights, MN: Apex
  Editions, 2022.

ONLINE RESOURCES

Visit **www.apexeditions.com** to find links and resources
related to this title.

ABOUT THE AUTHOR

Brienna Rossiter is a writer and editor who lives in
Minnesota.

INDEX

ANSWER KEY:
1. Answers will vary; 2. Answers will vary; 3. A; 4. A; 5. C; 6. B